CHAOS: A Wake-Up Call for Lightworkers

We Have Been Preparing For This For Decades

The Time To Serve Is Now

Kimberly Maska

Published and distributed in the United States by Spiritual Biz Publishing, Inc.

ISBN 978-1-950756-05-6 PAPERBACK
ISBN 978-1-950756-00-1 HARDCOVER
ISBN 978-1-950756-04-9 (Amazon Print)

The author of this book does not dispense medical advice, or prescribe the use of any technique as a form of treatment for physical, emotional, or medical problems without the advice of a physician, either directly or indirectly. The author of this book does not dispense financial advice. The intent of the author is only to offer information of a general nature to help you in your quest for emotional, financial, and spiritual well-being. In the event you use any of the information in this book for yourself, the author and publisher assume no responsibility for your actions.

Library of Congress Cataloging-in-Publication Data

Names: Kimberly Maska, author

Title: CHAOS: A Wake-Up Call for Lightworkers We Have Been Preparing for This for Decades The Time to Serve is Now / Kimberly Maska

Description: 1st Edition. | Asheville, North Carolina: Spiritual Biz Publishing, Inc., 2020

Subjects: Business | Spirituality

Spiritual Biz
PUBLISHING

The publisher for authors dedicated to shifting consciousness.

For more of our products visit spiritualbizpublishing.com

Table of Contents

I dedicate this work to all of those who have been severely impacted by this pandemic; financially, emotionally, and physically. To all the souls who were taken to the other side during the time of the Coronavirus, I wish you peace and hope you feel the love from those who are still in this dimension.

MY INTENTION

MY INTENTION IS to inspire you into action!

I believe the epidemic we're currently facing is a wake-up call for Lightworkers to take action. In fact, epidemics have always awakened the light within spiritual leaders—only this time, one of those leaders happens to be YOU! That's right, if you've been sitting on the fence, wondering if you're ready to lead, the time has come to stop wondering and start taking decisive action.

This is no longer about you. This is about helping to raise the vibration of the planet and courageously leading those who are unable to cope with the current situation. This is about serving!

You made an agreement with Source before you came into this density. You knew the role you were going to play, and while you may have forgotten the details, I am here to refresh your memory.

It is your duty to assist others in times of crisis. This is what you have been training for during your own awakening process. You experienced the pain, loss, and grief in your own awakening so you could guide people to find inner peace.

In this book, I will provide you with the first steps necessary to jump-start your spiritual business and inspire you to use your business as a vehicle to serve. Not only will you glean valuable information, but if you're committed to taking action, I'm certain the information in this book can change your life.

The phrase, "take action" is not to be taken lightly. You see, I expect you to *do* something with the information I'm giving you. This is not a book to be read and put back on the self. This is a book to be acted upon.

Throughout this book, you will find different ways to take action with various exercises and specific links to free trainings. There is no obligation, except for the one you have to yourself for sharing your gifts with the world. This is how I serve, and quite honestly, how you should be serving as well.

If that bothers you, then it may be beneficial to do some inner work and discover why you are bothered. Listen to your body and feel where the resistance is located. Is it in your upper chest, stomach, throat? Your body is trying to tell you something; listen to it and expand from this experience.

Now let's begin...

"It is your duty to assist others in times of crisis."
#WakeUpCall
@KimberlyMaska

INTRODUCTION

I DON'T WATCH "the news." I always thought it was rather pompous of the media to call it "the news," instead of "some news." Clearly, there is more than one perspective when it comes to planetary events. Anyway, I digress.

Since I don't watch the news, I rely on alternative sources, in addition to a few key people in my life who bring important things to my attention. When the Coronavirus outbreak was confined to other countries, it seemed unreal and far away. Then it came to the United States, and as I write this, my quaint little town of Asheville, North Carolina is on lockdown. It is very surreal.

It has occurred to me, as I have watched the shelves go bare and the stores close, that panic didn't come from the gnosis within each person, but was caused by something outside of themselves—mostly the media. The fear-mongering media is working overtime. Millions of people are terrified, not only of what is happening today, but of what might happen over the next three months, six months, or full year from now. That is an awfully big burden to carry: to worry about what might happen in a year.

I called my dad a couple of days ago; he lives all of three minutes from us, and his vibration was incredibly low when he answered the phone. I thought something was seriously wrong because I had spoken to him less than twenty-four hours before, and he was happy and cheerful. Turns out he had spoken to his sister, and the epidemic at hand was the topic of the conversation. By the time I spoke to him, he was depressed—overwhelmed by what was happening in the world. It took me a good ten minutes to get him back in alignment, but then I thought, "What about all the people who don't have someone to snap them out of this?"

Most of the world is not prepared for what we are experiencing. They are easily impacted by the media, stories from friends, and worrisome thoughts shared by family members. People around the globe are falling prey to low-vibration emotions like fear, panic, and anxiety. They have not learned how to properly balance between order and chaos, or, as spiritual entrepreneurs like to say, "Maintain a high vibration."

There is a clear distinction between being afraid and being aware. When we "react" with fear, we diminish our connection with Source Energy; however, when we "respond" out of pure awareness, we receive gnosis, which is divine guidance. The more I observed the crisis situation, the more I realized that the masses are reacting while few are responding. That is when it became clear to me. This is a challenge, or better yet, a test! A test for all of us. The introduction of this virus is pushing on our emotional boundaries to see how evolved we have become. This book was written in response to the

"Coronavirus" epidemic, but it could have been written during any crisis—any instance of chaos we have faced. Globally or individually.

Those who refuse to awaken will primarily align themselves with fear, surrender their individual sovereignty, and fall short of passing the test. This is why it is vitally important that the Lightworkers of the world be strong enough to balance between chaos and order.

After all, we have been preparing for this for decades, and we should be ready. All of the shadow work, all of our awakening experiences have been preparing us for this exact moment.

We mustn't confuse the word "test" with the word "judgment." We are not being judged. We are, however, being tested. Indeed, the Universe is delivering a test so humanity can begin to discern the difference between high- and low-vibrational frequencies. So you see, it is essential that we pass. Those who fall short will remain in an unawakened state for an extended period of time, while those who rise to the occasion and pass the test will become spiritual leaders who teach others how to master their own vibrations. How will we pass, you ask? By enhancing our "receptive mode" and relying solely upon our internal knowing. In essence, we must trust our connection with Source while maintaining a heightened sense of awareness of the 3D occurrences.

I was inspired to write this book to make sure we pass this test with flying colors. So inspired, in fact, that I wrote it in less than two weeks. I knew I had to share this message; this is our time to show the world what we can do as a collective consciousness of Lightworkers.

"This virus is pushing our emotional boundaries
to see how evolved we have become."
#WakeUpCall
@KimberlyMaska

WHO THIS BOOK IS FOR

If you made it this far, I am pretty sure this book is for you. But just in case, let's double-check. Are you a Lightworker, healer, empath, starseed, spiritual teacher, or coach? Do you know you were put here on this earth to help others to evolve?

Do you *know* in every cell of your body that you have a gift to share with the planet?

Have you been thinking about starting your own spiritual business? Or maybe you're someone who already has a few clients but feels a little overwhelmed with the prospect of having a thriving spiritual business because you have no idea where to start?

I can see you nodding your head.

Humanity needs spiritual leaders right now, and that means you. That also means it's time for you to take the necessary steps to create your spiritual business so you can serve today.

Not only should you be serving others, but you should also be serving yourself by creating a business where you are in charge of your own income, your own schedule, and your own life.

Right now, people across the country are experiencing layoffs because someone else is in charge of their income and employment. I was in our local coffee shop just before the lockdown, and the woman in front of me was talking about how fifteen people were laid off from her company that day. She was one of the lucky ones who got to stay, at least for another week.

When you are an entrepreneur, you are in charge of your income. Part of what I teach in my Spiritual Biz Bootcamp program is how to create money independently of what the 3D world is showing you. This way you are no longer held hostage by the corporate structures on this planet.

So if you want to know how to make your spiritual business profitable, how to make it all work so that you can live your purpose and serve on this planet, then you are in exactly the right place, and this book will change your life.

When people join Spiritual Biz Bootcamp, they come in thinking they are going to learn how to build their businesses, and they do. But they also experience inner transformation and spiritual renewal during their twelve weeks with me and my team.

This is not only something I teach but something I had to learn as well. Building a successful spiritual business allowed me to step out as a spiritual leader, but it also created a massive shift and allowed me to transcend my limiting beliefs.

The same will happen to you as you start to create a professional spiritual business platform. It's extremely important to be prepared for these shifts because as soon as they begin, our conditioned-belief system pushes back.

In the beginning, it can feel rather daunting to shift our beliefs because... well, because it's a bit scary to shift beliefs. We are not only changing ourselves, but we are changing how the world perceives us, and our ego dreads the fact that not everyone will be on board. Our brain begins to think about all the friends and family members who are going to think we are crazy. We "fear" these people will never be able to see us in our new light, and this creates a big vibrational wobble within ourselves.

To help you transcend these fears and show you how to create a successful spiritual business, I have broken this book into two parts. The first part, entitled "Awakening," focuses on the spiritual growth you need to step out as a spiritual leader. We will check in to see where you are vibrationally, and I will give you some steps to get you solid so you can step out as a powerful being.

We will cover:

- How to integrate the 5D and 3D. Being able to master our 5D vibration while having 3D experiences can be a challenge. I will show you how to integrate the two.
- Be an alchemist of fear and limiting beliefs. When we can transmute fear and transcend limiting beliefs, we can operate at our highest potential.
- Why this critical time in history is our call to action. They need us and they need us now.

In the second part, entitled "Serving," we will dive into the steps you need to jump-start your spiritual business today so you can serve tomorrow. You will learn:

- Why your biggest opportunity for growth as a spiritual entrepreneur is learning how to successfully integrate the 3D world with your 5D awareness. This is a big struggle for the spiritually awakened, isn't it? We start looking around at the 3D and it doesn't match our vision. We're going to talk about that opportunity for growth.
- How to find and connect with your tribe. No more connecting with people who either don't want to pay you for your spiritual knowledge, or they say they don't need the transformation you provide. If you're having trouble connecting with clients, it's because you don't have a soul connection with your tribe.

- How to create money vs. earning it. Why you must learn to create so you can break free from the 3D.
- How to build a strong email list and the importance of doing so. I'm going to tell you right now that your email list is money in the bank, and many of us skip that step too often.
- Why you aren't serving if you aren't selling. Sometimes free is too expensive.

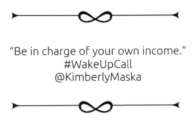

"Be in charge of your own income."
#WakeUpCall
@KimberlyMaska

Give Yourself A Gift

The content in this book will change your spiritual business, so give yourself a gift by dedicating time to read the book and take action on the steps I give you. This is for you to learn and expand because the world needs you right now. Indeed, the world needs you to step up and get out there with your spiritual business.

I also need you to remain open to receiving new information, which includes talking about success, money, and spirituality in the same breath. When we're new to creating a spiritual business, we tend to wobble in these areas, but

I'm going to bring it all together and show you how to maintain a steady vibration. You're going to discover how it all works together and hear about some extraordinary spiritual entrepreneurs who are putting their spiritual gifts to good use.

WHY THIS BOOK IS FOR YOU

BECAUSE YOU ARE A LIGHTWORKER AND THE WORLD NEEDS YOU NOW.

If you think having a profitable, spiritual business is too good to be true, I'm going to tell you straight out, you're wrong. It absolutely is possible; however, there's one small problem that keeps most spiritual entrepreneurs from experiencing genuine success.

You're probably asking yourself, "What's the problem?" The problem is that you haven't successfully integrated the 5D with the 3D.

This is especially true for the newly awakened. You have this amazing new 5D awareness, and thus, all things 3D no longer feel in alignment with who you have become.

But don't worry. We are going to be spending a lot of time discussing what I call "5D-3D integration." Once you're fully integrated, you will be aligned with your destiny and feel the excitement and joy of fulfilling your purpose. There's no other way to do it, and even if there was, why would you want to? Being in full alignment, both spiritually and professionally, is without a doubt the best way to create a successful business while maintaining the highest level of integrity.

IN CASE YOU DON'T KNOW WHO I AM

If you don't know me already, I'm Kimberly Maska. We have a lot to cover so I don't want to take up a lot of time talking about myself, but do know it is my soul purpose to show spiritual entrepreneurs how to keep their 5D vibration while creating 3D success. Yes indeed, my sole purpose is to integrate the esoteric with the physical here on this planet so that you can achieve success and change lives.

After working with hundreds of spiritual entrepreneurs in my Spiritual Biz Bootcamp program, I have been able to identify one key characteristic that all of my most successful clients have in common. They have learned to successfully integrate the 5D with the 3D. Not to worry, there is an entire chapter dedicated to this very topic.

It is also my spiritual gift to "see" people's businesses. If I can see it, then I know it is possible for you.

If you want to know more about my story and how I went from Wall Street to seven-figure spiritual entrepreneur, pick up my international bestselling book, ***Are You A Spiritual Entrepreneur?***

In addition to Spiritual Biz Bootcamp, I have also created a publishing company for authors dedicated to shifting consciousness. The biggest crime in publishing is that authors are allowed to publish a book without having a proven method of monetizing and profiting from their work. In fact, most authors lose money when they publish a book, whether they work with a traditional publisher or they self-publish.

That is why I created <u>Spiritual Biz Publishing</u>, where I show you how to monetize your book and get it into the hands of those who need it most. I know my book, "Are You a Spiritual Entrepreneur?", has created at least $80,000 in income since it launched a few months ago. And I have no doubt it will continue to bring me prosperity over the next several years.

I have learned how to create abundance with my spiritual gifts, and I can show you how to do the same. Can you imagine the paradigm shift that will occur when the healers of the world are thriving financially? The masses are not going to know what to do with us – other than become inspired and follow in our footsteps.

"Can you imagine the paradigm shift that will occur when the healers of the world are thriving financially?"
#WakeUpCall
@KimberlyMaska

PART 1:
Awakening

1

Crisis As Part Of Our Spiritual Awakening

"I really do think that any deep crisis is an opportunity to make your life extraordinary in some way."

~ Martha Beck

I'M GOING TO just say this flat out: I believe this virus was given to us. It didn't suddenly appear out of nowhere. There was a plan, and it was introduced into our physical reality for a reason.

What is that reason?

Was it introduced to break down the economic system so we could rebuild it and get rid of the Federal Reserve? Possible.

Was it brought in so we could clear out a significant number of the population to control overcrowding?

Possible.

Was it brought in so that the government can declare a national state of emergency and take over things they don't normally have their hands in? Possible.

Is this part of a bigger plan that involves beings from different dimensions that are battling for Earth? Possible.

Is it here because all the systems as we know them need to be broken up (healthcare, schools, media, money, the political system)? Possible. Actually, I will go with probable here.

There are a million possibilities that we may never fully understand.

As we look at the planet right now, the 3D looks like it is in full chaos, does it not? And if you allow your vibration to drop, even for a second, it feels like it is in chaos too. It is exactly what certain negative entities want us to feel.

The reason it looks and feels like chaos is because we can't see the bigger picture; we are too close to it all. It is similar to looking at an Impressionist painting up close. What first looks like chaotic tiny brush strokes actually turn into the beautiful genius of Monet when we step back.

I believe what's happening right now is that we're so close to the situation at hand, it looks like chaos. The problem is we don't have a broad enough perspective to really understand what is happening. If we step back far enough, it may begin to look like complete order.

I believe that there is some truth to this because this crisis, like any crisis we experience, is part of the awakening process. We all talk about the "great awakening," and I am sure we all pictured something beautiful and glorious.

However, when the masses are slow to awaken, we need a push. And the introduction of this virus into our 3D reality is part of the push we need. This is the Universe's way of shaking everyone awake. Now, I don't think this was the intention of those who introduced the virus to us, but it is the outcome... if we take decisive action!

The awakening process is now happening at quantum speed. As the crimes against humanity are revealed, the awakening will accelerate and gain momentum, and we Lightworkers need to be ready to assist in any way we can.

So while we thought the "great awakening" was going to be beautiful and amazing, it instead looks like chaos.

I want to check in with you. Where are you in this 3D 'chaos'?

Because to step out as a spiritual leader, you have to learn to maintain your vibration and master your balance between order and chaos. Are you able to maintain your balance and your connection with Source? Are you able to be present regardless of what is happening around you?

Or do you find your vibration impacted by the people and media surrounding you?

If you find yourself slipping into a lower vibration, then we have to figure out how to shift you back to neutral. Because if you are sitting in fear, worry, stress, or anxiety, you're not serving anybody.

The whole point of being a spiritual leader is to be able to master your vibration. And since we are human, holding our vibration steady is our greatest challenge. The contrast we face today is a teaching tool for us to determine how connected we are with Source and our knowing that everything is as it should be.

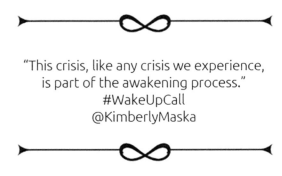

"This crisis, like any crisis we experience,
is part of the awakening process."
#WakeUpCall
@KimberlyMaska

WHERE IS YOUR VIBRATION?

Where is your vibration now? Are you conscious of where you hold your vibration? Or do you let external circumstances swing your vibration in all directions?

If you are feeling a tiny bit of fear, or even more than a tiny bit, that is okay. It is being highlighted in your reality so it can be addressed, and your awakening process can continue. The contrast can be used as a tool to expand your consciousness to the next level.

A common fear bubbling up right now is scarcity. You might be afraid of losing your job; with everything closing, furloughs are prevalent. Or just worried about money in general with what they did with the stock market, which was done to create more fear and panic, so it is understandable if that is what is bubbling up inside you. But let me ask you this, if your financial situation was in order, would you still be experiencing scarcity? Probably not.

If you are experiencing fear around finances, then this is telling you it is time to focus on getting your finances in order. What steps do you need to take to heal your relationship with money so that you aren't in this situation again in the future? I will help with that in the Serving section of the book. There is a Money Story exercise you can get access to in Chapter 8.

The same is true if you are experiencing fear around getting sick from the virus. Is your temple—your body—in order? Are you exercising and eating healthy so that your body and immune system are strong? We all know the steps we need to take to heal our bodies. So if this sounds like you, get on it ASAP.

Whatever fear you are experiencing, it means that you haven't taken care of yourself somehow. These fears are appearing so you can continue on your own healing journey and then share that experience with the world.

I was listening to an Eckhart Tolle video the other day, and he was talking about the structure of your house—your house being you. When your house is built on stone and made of stone, you can weather any storm. There is no worry, no fear, because you are solid. But when your house is built on sand and made of sand, the lightest wind can carry it away, and that creates worry.

How have you built your house? How is your temple? Where's your vibration?

If your house is built on sand, then you will continue to experience contrast until you stop and realize you need to build a stone house.

To step out as a spiritual leader, you need a stone foundation so you can hold your vibration steady, no matter what the 3D circumstances show you. Yes, as humans we will still have days that are off or we may react instead of respond to a situation, but a key element of a spiritual leader is that we are aware when it happens and are able to quickly course-correct.

The ability to quickly course-correct our vibration is what makes us leaders. We have to be able to hold our vibration steady and be role models for those who struggle with this balance. Most people don't have anywhere to look to for support. When they look around at their friends and family, they discover that they too are in the same low vibration. They are complaining, they're upset, they're worried, they're in fear, they're in scarcity. Like attracts like, as we know. They need leaders to show them the way out.

"The contrast we face today is a teaching tool for us
to determine how connected we are with Source."
#WakeUpCall
@KimberlyMaska

2

Integrating The 5D With The 3D Of The Virus

"Alignment trumps everything. Stay off the subject that disturbs your alignment, and everything that you are about will come into alignment."

~Abraham Hicks

WHEN I HEARD the word "terminal," all I wanted to do was hide. My emotions went from fear, to anger, back to fear. The doctor was telling my mom that she only had weeks to live. My body was still reeling with emotions when my mom turned to me and said, "I am going to be okay." It was almost as if she hadn't heard what the doctor had said.

You could look at this one of two ways: either she was in complete denial or in her own version of the 5D.

Ignoring the 3D cost her her life. She knew she was dying before they ever told her, but she disregarded all of the symptoms and warning signs.

I have been watching some spiritual beings on this planet do the same thing with the virus. They are saying, "This won't impact me." That is very Abraham-Hicks, and I love it. However, most humans can't hold that vibration long enough to make it their 3D reality. That's why most people can only manifest the exact amount of money they need — because they can't hold the vibration long enough to have consistent abundance. They get into alignment, the money they desire appears in their 3D reality, and then they drop their vibration, and the money ceases to flow in steadily.

Until we can master our vibration to the point where we transcend the 3D, we need to have 3D awareness.

"That's why most people can only manifest the exact amount of money they need — because they can't hold the vibration long enough to have consistent abundance."
#WakeUpCall
@KimberlyMaska

So how do we integrate the 5D and the 3D with the virus, or any crisis for that matter? Maintaining your highest-possible vibration is the first step. And only after we are in a high-vibrational state can we look at the 3D.

We need to be informed of what is happening, but we need to be solid in our mood before that occurs. Being solid then allows us to take in the 3D information through our 5D lens.

Let's talk about what it means to be informed. I am not talking about "the news." Sure you can peek in and see what they are talking about since you do need to know about things like school and store closures, but just remember the source of "the news."

Do your research beyond what the mainstream media is telling us. There are many, many theories on what's happening now—I mentioned a few at the beginning of this book. Go broaden your awareness so you aren't making assumptions from a place of ignorance. Be as informed as possible.

As with all information you receive, you need to double-check with your inner guidance. Tap into your higher self and feel into the information. How does it feel to you? If it feels out of alignment, double-check to make sure it isn't just bumping up against a limiting belief you have been carrying around. Then feel into it again at a core vibrational level, and you will see your truth. Always knowing that the answer is within.

Now integrate the 5D and 3D by taking your 5D gnosis and then determine what precautions you have to take in the 3D to keep safe. For example, take precautions in the 3D like buying food and basic necessities and keeping your distance from people you don't know, like you would in any flu season, but also use your inner guidance system. And if your inner guidance says you don't need to rush to the store for food, then don't.

Be smart about your choices. Question everything. Feel into everything. We can't yet see the final outcome of this, so be in alignment with YOU every step of the way.

"Until we can master our vibration to the point where we transcend the 3D, we need to have 3D awareness."
#WakeUpCall
@KimberlyMaska

3

Be An Alchemist Of Fear & Limiting Beliefs

"Don't give in to your fears. If you do, you won't be able to talk to your heart."

~ Paulo Coelho

"I AM SO worried. I read in the paper that the number of cases are tripling each day. I just can't believe this is happening; it is so horrible. I hear the nurses in the hospitals are terrified and crying, hiding in closets. They say it can last for eighteen months. What are we going to do?" Her eyes glistened with tears and fear behind her mask.

I just looked at her, sent her love from my heart, and smiled. I knew she was in too much fear to try to shift her while standing in line (almost six feet away for social distancing) for coffee. She was waiting for me to jump on her train and agree with her; because she was afraid, she wanted me to be afraid too. When I didn't join in her fear, she looked at me like something was wrong with me, and I could see a flint of anger in her eyes. How dare I not be afraid as well?

I understand she was afraid, but this is the classic example of someone trying to put their fear on us. They are trying to feed us, what my husband likes to call, a "sh!t sandwich" filled with fear. I don't know about you, but that is a sandwich I have no desire to consume.

Are you finding your family and friends, who have not yet awakened, following the same pattern? Somehow it makes them feel better to know others are afraid with them. This stems from our desire to belong, to not be outcasts. Sheeple feel safer in numbers.

People do this with their limiting beliefs all the time as well. Let's say you buy yourself something really nice that you have been wanting for a long time. It could be anything from a beautiful handbag to a vintage turntable. You share your exciting news with your mom, and she immediately says, "Why would you spend so much on [name of the item]. You should be saving your money, not spending it on silly things." In this scenario, she tried to feed you a scarcity "sh!t sandwich." Not only did she try to put her fear on you, but she tried to make you feel bad too. And when you don't agree with her, she becomes angry, getting louder to make her point.

It is funny how you turn into the "bad guy" because you won't take in their negative energy.

As a spiritual leader, you need to be a master alchemist of fear and limiting beliefs. You have to be so strong in your beliefs and your vibration that a scenario like the above doesn't rattle you.

You have to understand that their beliefs—their fears—have nothing to do with you; they have everything to do with what they are carrying around that must be healed within them. This is even true when someone is "offended" with something you say or do. Just because they are offended does not make it your problem.

Now, admittedly, we always need to do an internal check and be 100 percent responsible for our actions. But if you are in alignment with your actions, and someone has an issue with you, then you are free to transmute the energy of their fear and limiting beliefs into something useful.

I actually had a scenario like the above happen to me recently. A "spiritual person" reached out, angry that I was calling Lightworkers forward to step up and then offering a program to help them do so. What's ironic is I took my high-end Spiritual Biz Bootcamp program, automated it, and then offered the content at one sixteenth of the regular price. I am in full alignment with how I am serving, so I know this completely belongs to her.

Learn to be a master alchemist. Be an alchemist of fear by shifting the energy into excitement. For the woman I met in line waiting for coffee, I could have responded to her fear by saying, "Think about how amazing it will feel when this is all over." I could have transmuted her fear into excitement about the future. She may not have shifted her energy to match mine, but it keeps me from dropping to her low vibration.

Be prepared with responses to situations so you can *respond* instead of *react*. Being prepared is one of the best ways to hold your vibration. Since you already know your response, you can just reach for it with no emotional attachment to what the other person has said.

Some great examples of high-vibration responses include:

"I am choosing not to take part in your reality."

"You enjoy your reality and I will enjoy mine."

"Enjoy your reality as you are its creator."

"I believe that you believe that to be true."

Admittedly, these phrases could be said with a low-vibration tone, so be careful. Just as the words, "I'm sorry" can be said with such feeling that you know in your heart the person truly is sorry, or they can be said with such disdain that there is no positive meaning behind them, so can these phrases. Come from a place of love as you speak them. And preface them with, "I hear you," so that the person you are speaking with can feel your connection with them.

My response to the woman who wrote me, angry with how I was serving, was this: "I hope you can hear this message… clearly this has triggered you, which is great. See this as an opportunity to heal something that has been left unchecked and expand as a spiritual being. This is exactly what I have been talking about… this whole Coronavirus thing is a trigger to heal us and move us closer to our purpose. Enjoy your reality as you are its creator."

Have fun creating your responses. The key is to be prepared so you have a response and not a reaction connected to emotion.

One last thing before we move on: no guilt! I have seen a couple of spiritual leaders feel the tiniest bit guilty about feeling at complete peace during this time even though the 3D dictates otherwise. They are watching everyone around them in panic and fear and slip a little into "feeling bad" for their family and friends. You can never feel bad enough to help someone. The only answer is to stay in your highest vibration and bring them up to meet you.

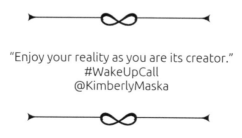

"Enjoy your reality as you are its creator."
#WakeUpCall
@KimberlyMaska

4

This Pandemic Is Our Call To Action

"I've been impressed with the urgency of doing. Knowing is not enough; we must apply. Being willing in not enough: we must do."

~ Leonardo Da Vinci

CLEARLY, THIS IS not a situation anyone would want in their reality (except for the people who created it and introduced it to us), but since it is here, we have to determine our roles.

How are you going to show up during these uncertain times? How are you going to serve people, like my father, who have not yet learned to master their vibrations and are being emotionally impacted by everything going on?

If you think about it, it is actually your duty to step out and serve with the gifts that Source has given you. This is a time to step up and step out.

I know many of the Lightworkers I have come into contact with are feeling this urgency—the urgency to serve.

If you are being overwhelmed by this sense of urgency as well, then let me ask you this... how much energy are you putting into your business so you can reach more people?

It is one thing to serve your friends and neighbors, and it is something entirely different to help globally. How are you showing up for yourself and your business so that you can get your message out to those who need it most?

"How are you going to show up during
these uncertain times?"
#WakeUpCall
@KimberlyMaska

BE AN ALCHEMIST OF THE PANDEMIC

We were just talking about being alchemists of fear, so how are we going to be alchemists of this pandemic?

This is a huge opportunity for Lightworkers, and I am actually quite excited by it. People need what you have to offer: peace, joy, inner alignment. And as the awakening progresses, the demand for finding one's authentic self is increasing every day. It is simple supply and demand. There is a high demand for what you heal, so supply it!

Now, I know someone reading this will slip into a low vibration and think, "OMG, she is teaching us how to prey on people."

If this is you, then feel your way through it. Somewhere there is a limiting belief around, "If you want to serve, then it must be for free." That means what I am about to cover is going to bring some contrast into your reality. Where is the resistance coming up in your body? And better yet, where did you pick up that limiting belief? I highly doubt you created that belief on your own. I bet you you picked it up from someone else and it just stuck with you. Take control of your beliefs and make sure they are your own.

There was a post recently in my Spiritual Biz Success Facebook group from a woman who felt like she should be giving her services away for free or at a discount because of her 3D situation, and she was asking for my advice.

Let's think this through for a second... how exactly does that help anybody? When you give your services away for free, that puts you in scarcity because you are no longer receiving abundance, all because you feel sorry for others. And when you feel sorry for someone, that means you are no longer seeing them as a child of Source, but you are seeing them as a low-vibration, helpless person.

When we move to giving our services away for free, then we stop the energy flow of money. And then what happens? We start to hoard money because there "might not be enough," and we begin to suffocate it. Then it stops flowing to us because we are in scarcity and have stopped the flow of money. If you don't receive money, then you stop tithing, and you stop going to eat at your local restaurants, which means your favorite server no longer gets her tips. We cannot stop the flow of money. They stopped the flow by closing down all the "non-essential" businesses and it is creating an economic crisis.

Which leads me to this, if there was ever a time to continue tithing, this would be it. (If you want to know more about tithing as a spiritual entrepreneur, I cover it in detail in my book, *Are You a Spiritual Entrepreneur?*). Therefore, you must keep the energy of money flowing, keep your business running, and keep charging.

It helps nobody to give your services away for free. Now, can you create free gifts that are not tied to your time? ABSOLUTELY, and you should. But don't give away your services. Do you see the difference? Your services are directly tied to your time, while your free gifts are not.

As an entrepreneur, you have to make sure that your core business is intact so you aren't suffocating the energy of money.

This is also how you will be a role model for other spiritual entrepreneurs. They will say, "Wow, this person really held their vibration. How did they manage to succeed at a time like this?" If you think about it, in every crisis, in every depression, there are still plenty of people who *create* money.

So how do we create money? There is a whole chapter dedicated to creating money in the second half of this book. Just know it is about serving at the highest level. When you can serve people and change their lives, they will seek you out, and you will always be abundant.

Just as a side note, I know part of my role in this paradigm shift is to trigger you. I am here to shift limiting beliefs around spirituality and money to get you to think differently. So when I trigger someone, it is kind of exciting because I know I am moving stagnant energy around.

I hold each of you in the highest light and can see your full potential. When your limiting beliefs get in the way of your full potential, I don't allow it. I don't allow some old story to keep you from being extraordinary, and you shouldn't either. There is no room for mediocre spiritual leaders.

"When we move to giving our services away for free,
then we stop the energy flow of money."
#WakeUpCall
@KimberlyMaska

5

Are You Being Irresponsible?

*"God does not have any business with
irresponsible people."*

~ Sunday Adelaja

IF YOU AREN'T living your purpose, you are being
irresponsible.

If you aren't in your joy the majority of the time, you
are being irresponsible.

If you are making money in a nine to five that is
sucking your soul dry, you are being irresponsible.

If you are living a mediocre life, like the rest of the
sheeple, you are being irresponsible.

I could go on, but you get my point.

You are being irresponsible to the world because you
are not in your highest vibration. You have compromised

your vibration to be part of the 3D world. It's not the fault of the 3D world, you just need to master your 5D vibration while being part of the 3D experiences.

You are being irresponsible to yourself because you were not put on this planet to struggle, suffer, or be in a low vibration.

You are being irresponsible to your family. Your family deserves to have the best version of you available to them. If you are not in your joy, then you are passing that less-than-desirable vibration on to your family. It is not fair to them.

And think about it, why would you want to introduce "mediocre" into the world? The world needs more extraordinary people, not mediocre people.

So if your life is anything less than extraordinary, you are being irresponsible.

Are you ready to be responsible?

"If you aren't living your purpose, you
are being irresponsible."
#WakeUpCall
@KimberlyMaska

Part 2:

Serving

6

5D Vibration With 3D Success

"I challenge you to make your life a masterpiece. I challenge you to join the ranks of those people who live what they teach, who walk their talk."

~ Tony Robbins

ONCE YOU'VE HAD your awakening, and you understand the 5D, it's a challenge to come back to the 3D, isn't it? It's a little uncomfortable. We've gone through this awakening—we've had this amazing 5D experience; however, our newfound awareness brings the falsehoods of the 3D into perspective. You know what I'm talking about? You can now see the sheeple and think, *Oh my goodness, I was once a sheeple. Oh, what the heck?*

We now see the sheeple, how society has been set up to control us with "the news," TV, banks, debt, pharmaceuticals. It's all there to keep us in a very specific little box, isn't it?

But now that we're awake, we can see how important it is for others to wake up as well. You feel the urgency behind sharing your new knowledge with the world, don't you? You want to wake people up and say, "Can't you see what they're doing to us?"

Here is the issue I have seen with the newly awakened. We have a new lens to see the world through, and since it makes us more aware of what's going on, we develop an underlying disdain for anything 3D. We see what's going on and we don't like it.

Then we start to allow 3D stuff to rub us the wrong way. Things like money, marketing, and sales begin to turn us off. We begin to have disdain for the 3D, and I gotta be honest, this is where the spiritual *want*repreneurs fail. And I know that's a tough one to swallow, but this is exactly where it happens.

It's because they simply don't understand that the real test of being on Planet Earth is to integrate—to integrate the 5D with the 3D. If everything is 5D, it's all just airy fairy and nothing gets done and it really doesn't serve anyone. We have to integrate the 3D because we're currently living on a 3D planet, we are on Earth. We don't really have a choice about it.

Here's what the successful integration looks like to me: When you successfully integrate, you can hold your 5D vibration while manifesting 3D success.

Like I said, this is where spiritual wantrepreneurs fail. They try to push away the 3D, and they're just going to sit and meditate and tell everybody how amazing things are and hope that they follow them along on the same path. That doesn't work.

You have to integrate into the 3D so that you can truly serve. The integration is part of the spiritual journey.

So you see, when you successfully integrate as a professional spiritual entrepreneur, you begin to have a big impact on the planet. You get to show others how it works, not by telling them, but by being a living example. You get out there, you create a business to serve, and then you create abundance.

When you are fully integrated, you serve at the highest level, and the money *flows* to you. You can create abundance to give back out into the world, which can have an amazing impact. And that is when you become a role model for the people who want a spiritual business but are feeling resistance around integrating the 3D with the 5D to find success.

Now, you may be thinking, *But wait, didn't you just say the banking system is set up to control us and that includes money?* Yeah. Yeah, I did. You're right. I did say that. And I do believe it's a control system; however, it's not going away, at least anytime soon.

In the current state, from what we know today, we need money here in the 3D. As spiritual entrepreneurs and leaders, we must learn how to win the game by first learning how to play the game... and believe me, it's all a game.

We can either choose to play the game to win or complain about the game and struggle with it. We can struggle with money and everything else that's in the 3D or we can choose to master the ability to create money. Now, *creating* money is different than *earning* money. So let's talk about the difference.

"You have to integrate the 5D with the 3D
so you can truly serve."
#WakeUpCall
@KimberlyMaska

7

Creating Money

"If you make meaning, you'll make money."

~ Guy Kawasaki

LET'S TALK ABOUT *creating* money. This is a very different concept than *earning* money. I am going to define the terms here so we are on the same page.

When someone earns money, they are exchanging their time or labor for the energy of money. You probably fall into one of two scenarios. In the first scenario, a company pays you a fixed annual salary in expectation that you will work the standard nine to five at a minimum and that you complete the tasks they give you each day. As long as you meet or exceed their expectations, and the company is profiting, you will get paid.

The second alternative is that you earn your money hourly. You may get paid $35 an hour, and you are only paid if you are physically present at your place of work. If you are sick and need to take a day off, you don't earn money.

In both of these scenarios, you are dependent on a company to pay you for your time. They "give" you a paycheck and can decide not to give you one at their own discretion. This is earning money.

When you earn money, you are at risk of financial peril because you're relying on other people for your income. And do you want to know the saddest part about this? You're completely tied to the very 3D you have been trying to escape because you're stuck in this system to get your money.

I remember once when I was about twelve years old, my parents were in a tight financial situation. I can't say I remember the exact details, but I could see the desperation in my mom's eyes about not knowing how to get money. See, she only knew how to *earn* money, so she started applying for jobs. It seemed at the time that she was applying and getting rejected an awful lot. If I remember correctly, it took some time, but she eventually got one, and we managed to get by. But her fear around money never left her.

What she was missing, and I bet what you are missing too, is the understanding of how to *create* money. Creating money entails tapping into your creative abilities—your connection with Source.

Have you ever gotten an idea about something—a book to write, a product to create, a new invention—but then didn't act on it? Well, that was you tossing your creative ability out the window.

You might be thinking, *But I am not creative.* That is a limiting belief you are carrying around. Who told you you weren't creative? Probably someone trying to keep you from your greatness. Forgive them and let's move on.

You all have a God-given gift to be able to create. You just have to get past your limiting beliefs about what it means to be creative. Begin to ponder, what kind of business can I create? What can I do to create abundance? You all have the ability to do it. There's not one of you out there who can say, "I don't know how to create." You are arguing for your limitations if you truly believe that.

To tap into our creative abilities, we need to ask Source for guidance. As Abraham-Hicks says, "Ask and you shall receive." Source will deliver the idea to you, always. You just need to be in the receptive mode so you can hear it and act on it. In fact, even when you aren't "asking," Source is delivering ideas to you all the time. You just aren't acting on them. Deep down, you know what you should be doing on this planet; you know how you should be serving. Source is giving you this information every day, but you're not taking action.

Since you aren't taking action on the inspiration you are receiving, you aren't creating money. You're keeping yourself stuck in the 3D matrix of having to go earn your money at a regular nine-to-five job.

But when you learn to create, you're in control. You can be in control of your income, you can be in control of your life, you can be in control of your career, and you can be in control of your money. When you learn to tap into your creative abilities, you can take that 5D information you're getting from Source, activate it, and put it into action, so you can manifest it into the 3D and can see it in your reality. *That's* the integration you need.

I have mentioned it already: my most successful clients have learned how to integrate the 5D with the 3D. They understand they can use the tools of the 3D—the tools like money, marketing, sales, and having a business—to spread their 5D message.

And they do it very successfully. They take the 5D information they get from their connection with Source and bring it down into the 3D and ground it there so they can manifest it into this reality and succeed. When you can consistently do this—be an integrated soul—that is when you become a spiritual leader and can experience 3D success while being in a 5D vibration and stop struggling on this planet.

While those are the steps, you will achieve your greatest success when you find ways to serve people. When you provide an amazing service to people who really need and want it, you will always be in abundance. So how are you going to serve?

Here is a little exercise for you: in tomorrow morning's meditation, ask Source for inspiration on what you can create so that you can serve on this planet. Meditate and go on with your day. Don't rush the process. Allow Source to deliver, and be ready to receive the information. Pay attention to the signs and you will find your answer.

"Creating money entails tapping into your creative abilities – your connection with Source."
#WakeUpCall
@KimberlyMaska

SLIPPING INTO SCARCITY

I HAD A conversation with a client shortly after all this started, and she had completely slipped into scarcity. She is in the very beginning stages of creating her program and, with everything going on, she started to think, *Oh my God, everything's closed; people have been laid off and don't have money. How am I going to create my business if no one has money to pay me?*

She went right down the scarcity rabbit hole. I helped her reframe the situation, and I hope this brings you clarity and assurance that stepping out right now is the best time ever for spiritual entrepreneurs.

I told her that yes, things might appear chaotic, but you are in the best spot because people need what you have to offer, which is peace, joy, and a deeper connection with themselves and Source.

When people need and want what you have to offer, they will do an energy exchange in the form of money with you. You know what is amazing about this client? She actually helps parents gain deeper relationships with themselves so they can be more connected with their families. And with parents being home with their kids for weeks or months, anything that hasn't been healed in that relationship will bubble to the top. The parents are going to absolutely need what she has to offer, and they are going to want it now to save their sanity.

When I flipped it for her, she responded with, "Oh my God, you're right." Her timing is perfect, and so is yours.

So if somewhere in the back of your mind you are thinking that money is tight, realize that is the 3D reality you are creating. But you can transcend that 3D reality when you are in vibrational alignment with creating money and serving people. People are looking for help.

Plus, there is an infinite amount of money in this world. We can't even get our heads around how much money and abundance there is. If scarcity continues to creep into your thoughts, add this to your meditation: "God is my infinite supply." It works like a charm.

So, start thinking about how you will serve. How can you stand out in your field so that people look at your offering and say, "I need that"? It really is the perfect time, the perfect storm for Lightworkers to step out with their creative abilities.

Stay focused on this goal and let nothing distract you from an extraordinary life. Stop watching the news. Stop reading the newspaper. Stop talking to your family if you have to. Get rid of all low-vibration influences so you can remain focused.

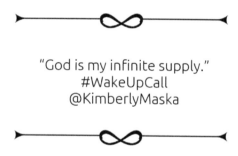

"God is my infinite supply."
#WakeUpCall
@KimberlyMaska

8

Fill In The Blank: Money Is

_____

"Money is life energy that we exchange and use as a result of the service we provide to the Universe."

~ Deepak Chopra

BEFORE YOU READ any further, write down your response. What is money to you?

This was the topic of conversation in my Spiritual Biz Success Facebook Group not too long ago. I was not at all surprised to see well over a hundred comments since any conversation about money seems to get a lot of attention. The vibration of the comments was all over the place as people brought their beliefs—some good, some limiting— to the table.

There was everything from "my friend," "energy," "not real," to the "root of all evil," "3D B.S. literally ink on paper," "a blessing for some a curse for myself," and "worthless."

It breaks my heart when I see people carrying around limiting beliefs about money.

To truly serve as spiritual entrepreneurs, we must get into alignment with money. You have awakened spiritually, and now it is time to awaken financially.

"To truly serve as spiritual entrepreneurs,
we must get in alignment with money."
#WakeUpCall
@KimberlyMaska

MONEY IN THIS 3D WORLD

Whether we like it or not, we need money in this 3D world. If we want to thrive and have an impact on the planet, then we have to insert ourselves in the 3D. Unless they completely flip the money system over during this Coronavirus epidemic, the game needs to be played by all spiritual leaders.

We need money for food, for clothes, and to put a roof over our heads. When we shun money, we are vibrationally pushing it away. While it would be amazing to live in a vibrational reality where there was complete abundance and no need for money, we aren't there yet.

I received an email from someone just the other day, and she was saying how she wished we didn't have a money system, and she was wishing it and all of the banks away. Without knowing much about this person, I would guess that she is financially stressed because she is repelling money away with every thought. If you are struggling financially and cursing the system, then, well, do I have to spell it out for you? Abundance will elude you.

Then there are the people who say, "I don't need it that much; I don't need much money to get by." That is one of the most selfish statements I have ever heard. By telling the Universe, "I don't need that much," you're actually giving up your responsibility as a human being on this planet to do good, aka you are being irresponsible.

Because when we have abundance, we're able to transform the world with quantum speed. We're able to feed families around the globe (assuming it's a globe). We're able to save the puppies from being euthanized. We're able to send clean water to the other side of the world. We're able to do things with money to serve in this 3D world. When we don't have money, we greatly limit our ability to serve.

Plus, you are holding back the highest version of yourself when you say, "I don't need that much." You were put on this planet to *thrive*. Why would you live a mediocre life, saying you don't need much, when you could be the best version of you?

And how exactly does money make you the best version of you? When you are abundant, it is easier to maintain a high vibration because you aren't stressed about money, you are able to donate money and help people, which releases a chemical known as oxytocin in the brain, thus making you feel good and raising your vibration, and you are able to expand as an individual by working with spiritual teachers, traveling the world, and having new experiences.

Are you seeing now why you must have a solid and positive relationship with money to serve on this 3D planet?

"By telling the Universe, 'I don't need that much,'
you're actually giving up your responsibility as a
human being on this planet to do good."
#WakeUpCall
@KimberlyMaska

MONEY AS CONTROL

I think our biggest issue with money is that we feel controlled by it, and rightly so since that is how it has been set up. No one likes to be conscious of being controlled, so we resist and drop our vibrations around money and the system that has created it.

We are not only controlled by the money system, but we have been conditioned with a set of limiting beliefs around money, particularly that money is bad or evil.

Poor money, it gets such a bad rap. It's not that money is bad, it's the people using the money. Let's look at a chair for example. A chair is generally made of wood. It is very useful to sit on while you are working. It can be a friendly sight after hours of standing. A chair is neither good nor bad, it is just a thing.

However, someone could take a chair, just like the one described above, and bludgeon someone with it, taking their life. Is the chair bad or evil? No. But the person using the chair is.

The same is true with money. It is neither good nor bad. It absorbs the energy of the person using it. Money in the hands of Lightworkers can be put to great use, which is why it is so important for Lightworkers to be wealthy.

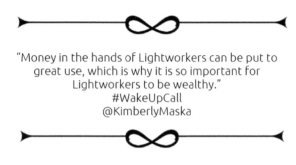

"Money in the hands of Lightworkers can be put to
great use, which is why it is so important for
Lightworkers to be wealthy."
#WakeUpCall
@KimberlyMaska

WHAT IS MONEY?

First, what is it? Is it paper? Plastic? Gold? When was the last time you actually touched paper money? We don't seem to use paper money much anymore. In fact, lately, I have been hearing in the media how "dirty" money is. It is almost like they don't want us touching it at all.

Most of the time, money is just the energy of numbers floating through the ether as we use debit cards and credit cards to move "money" from one place to another.

It truly is energy. We don't see it. We hardly touch it. And nobody really knows what it is anymore. It's not even backed by gold to give it value like it had before 1971. Now they just print it at their own free will. The $2 trillion stimulus package? Where exactly is the money coming from? But I digress.

At the end of the day, money is energy, as is everything else on this planet.

As spiritual leaders, we get to choose what kind of energy we want to put into money and determine how we will use it.

Here is a quote from Albert Einstein that will help clarify where I am going: "Everything is energy and that's all there is to it. Match the frequency of the reality you want, and you cannot help but get that reality. It can be no other way."

So, let's master our relationship with money instead of calling it the root of all evil, which, of course, it's not. It's only the energy that someone puts in it. If someone's going to put bad energy in it and use it for bad things, that's their energy. Which is why it's so important for spiritual leaders—spiritual entrepreneurs—to have money because we're the ones who can imbue money with love.

Put the energy of love into money and you will always be abundant. See money as a tool for accomplishing amazing things on this planet.

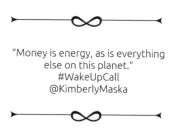

"Money is energy, as is everything
else on this planet."
#WakeUpCall
@KimberlyMaska

WHAT'S YOUR MONEY STORY?

Most people have been giving up their power to money since the day they were born. They have a story about money, and they live their entire lives perpetuating the story.

The crazy thing is, your money story probably isn't even your own story. Our money stories have been passed down to us before we even came into this dimension. Our ancestors' fears and beliefs around money are embedded in our cells. Then, growing up, our parents, family, and friends unknowingly passed their own beliefs on to us. We carry lifetimes of money stories.

No matter where it came from, we have to realize that it isn't our story. The story you have today belongs to someone else.

Some of those beliefs might look like...

"Money is evil."

"You have to work hard for money."

"The rich are greedy bastards."

"Money changes people."

"I don't need that much."

"Being poor is virtuous."

We just discussed how money is energy, so we can conclude that all of these statements are false beliefs, right?

Begin to think about your current money story. And then take a look at the money you are earning now. If you have always earned the same amount, say $5,000 a month, and no matter what you do or try, you always earn around the same amount, then more than likely there are some money beliefs keeping you at the $5k.

When I hire a new enrollment coach for my team, I always ask them, "What is the most amount of money you have earned in a month?" Because no matter what number they tell me, I know it will be difficult for them to create an income greater than that number without doing some serious money story work.

If you want a six-figure spiritual coaching business, then you must have a high-vibration money story.

By consciously creating a new money story, you will shift your frequency so you can attract and be open to receiving the money you desire.

It is time to take control and master your relationship with money so you can be 100 percent responsible for your financial situation.

I have created a Money Story exercise to help you with this process. You can access it here:

www.awakeupcallforlightworkers.com

After you create a high-vibe money story, focus on your income. Actually, I take that back, be *obsessed* with your income. How can you create a greater income so that you can create abundance and give it back into the world to have a massive impact? That's where you should be focusing. How do you create that income? Hint: it's with your spiritual business.

"Your money story probably isn't even your story."
#WakeUpCall
@KimberlyMaska

9

Soul Connection

"Our souls speak a language that is beyond human understanding. A connection so rare the universe won't let us part."

~ Nikki Rowe

WHEN I HEAR someone say that Facebook ads don't work, or marketing doesn't work, or they just can't find people who want to pay for their services, I know for a fact that they're missing this piece of the puzzle. They are missing the soul connection with their tribe.

I believe that your tribe is made up of the souls you have connected with before, whether that was in a past life, different dimension, or different density. You've connected with them, they know you, and you will recognize each other in this dimension.

You know exactly what I am talking about... you meet somebody, and every cell in your body is telling you that you have known them before. They are part of your soul tribe.

Your soul tribe is waiting for you to step out. They're searching for you, but many times they cannot yet hear you or see you. If you haven't stepped out yet at all, well, then we know why they can't find you.

But what if you have been trying to get out there with your spiritual business and still can't seem to find your tribe? It is because you aren't speaking to them so they can hear you here in the 3D.

You have to know how to connect with their souls so they will intuitively know they are supposed to connect with you and work with you. It is this intimate soul connection that will allow you to pull in the tribe of lives you're going to change.

When you have a soul connection with your tribe, there are a few pretty interesting things that begin to happen.

First, since you are attracting them in, they kind of just show up. When you dial in the soul connection, and can speak so they can hear you, your tribe will literally show up, saying things like their guides said they had to work with you. They're attracted to you because they can *feel* the connection with you.

They also begin to see you as an authority because you're attracting them to you, using what I call "pull energy," where you are energetically calling them or pulling them toward you. You're not *chasing* down a client, you're *attracting* them to you, and they see you as an authority, and they want to invest with you. They truly do. Have you ever trained a puppy? If you want to catch the puppy, you don't chase it. You put your hand out with a treat to get the puppy come to you, and then it sees you as the head dog—the leader of the pack. When you chase the puppy, it will run away from you. Same idea with clients.

If you've been struggling with getting clients, and clients who want to pay for your services, this has been part of the problem. When you have that soul connection, and energetically pull them to you, they want to invest with you. And then I have to say, marketing and sales becomes super easy because you're a vibrational match with your tribe. All that icky stuff about marketing and sales—it goes away because there's a connection, and they're coming to you.

So now here's a little exercise for you to use to begin attracting your soul tribe. Spend time imagining them exactly where they are right now and how you can serve them. Bring them into your meditation in the morning. What does their life look like? What are they going through? What are they feeling? What are they experiencing and how can you serve them? Because when you know how you will serve your tribe, you will be able to connect with them.

Now, when I say serve, I am not talking about a modality. I would not tell someone I am going to serve them with Reiki. No. You will serve them by helping them heal something within themselves—something they want fixed.

As a gift for you, I am giving you access to the Healing Statement exercise that I teach in my Spiritual Biz Bootcamp. This exercise is the foundation for your spiritual business and it is life-changing when you can finally make that soul connection. You can gain access to it here: www.awakeupcallforlightworkers.com

When you establish a soul connection with your tribe, you will have lifelong clients. Without this connection, none of the marketing or sales stuff will ever work.

"Your tribe is made up of souls you have been connected to before, whether that's been a past life, different dimension, or different density."
#WakeUpCall
@KimberlyMaska

10

Your Email List Is Money In the Bank

"Email has an ability many channels don't: creating valuable, personal touches – at scale."

~ David Newman

I KNOW THIS doesn't sound very exciting. We have gone from talking about being an alchemist of fear to mastering our money vibration, to... building an email list. Feels flat even as I type it.

While it might not be as exciting as everything else we have discussed, it is yet another way to serve and to bring in abundance.

Having a strong email list will help strengthen your connection with your tribe, and it will increase your income, yet I see so many spiritual entrepreneurs skip this step.

Probably because it does involve some technical know how, but just a little. When you have a strong email list, it really equals money. So it is worth focusing on.

In the email marketing world, they say that an email list of 10,000 people is worth $10,000 a year, minimum. That may not sound like a lot, but when you consider that this is *passive* income, that's not so bad. I like to call this passive income, Making Money While You Meditate™. You create an offer (i.e. a program), automate this program, put the offer in an email sequence, and let it run. That is a bit simplified but you get the idea.

However, in order to Make Money While You Meditate™ you have to have a tribe and an email list for your tribe. I want to be clear that for this to work you need emails from your soul tribe. Never, I repeat, *never* buy an email list. While it may sound tempting because you can purchase 100,000 emails and have this massive mailing list, but it won't be from your tribe. You will be missing the soul connection with the people on the list.

When you build your email list right, with a tribe that wants to connect with you, your email list becomes an asset to your business. How? Not only will your list make you money, it will also help you gain exposure. When you want to get on a podcast or be part of a summit, they will always ask you, "How big is your email list?" They are looking for people with a minimum of a 5,000-person email list.

Five thousand might sound like a lot, but if you start building it now, smartly, you can make it happen. As a side note, when they ask about your list, this is different from *buying* a list. The idea with the podcasts and summits is that the person interviewing you is in the same genre as you, so some of your tribe will be in their audience and vice versa. It is one more way to find your soul tribe.

OK, so you have to build a 5,000-person email list. You might be wondering how exactly to accomplish this. I bet you are thinking, "Of course, it's with my newsletter on my website." Wrong. I will get to why in just a second. So if not with a newsletter, then what is the secret sauce? You're going to create an irresistible offer; in marketing terms, this is called a lead magnet. You may have heard of it before, but I like to call it an irresistible offer.

What it is, is a free gift, like the ones you see on people's websites. But it isn't just a free gift. It needs to be super irresistible if you plan on building a 5,000-person email list.

Let's look at what makes this free gift irresistible. First, they have to really want it. It can't be something you *think* they want, it has to be something they *really* want.

Second, it should solve a problem for them so that when they're done using it, they're like, "Wow, that was really cool." And because they think it's cool, they're going to want to work with you some more.

Third, it should deliver quick results. So an ebook is not an irresistible offer. They're never going to get through it, and they're never going to know how amazing you are as a coach, which, in turn, does not lead to a new client. If you are using an ebook as your free gift, you need to replace it ASAP.

When you create your irresistible offer, you want to make sure that they know how awesome you are at what you do so they can begin to consider working with you. Therefore, your irresistible offer needs to give them quick results, so that within a week or two, they've used it and seen a shift in themselves.

Back to your newsletter. Your newsletter is not irresistible. If you think about it, why would someone sign up for a newsletter? When are they really gonna read it? Do they even know what's in it for them? They don't likely even know what it is. So you've got to ask yourself, is this newsletter really serving my tribe? Does it solve a problem for them?

This is where most people miss the mark, they have the best intentions with their newsletter, but they forgot to ask themselves if it truly serves their tribe. I know I've done it—I am totally guilty of doing this in the past. I completely forgot to think about how it would actually change my tribe's life. It didn't, so I pulled it.

Everything we do should come from a place of service.

So if you have a newsletter on your website as an opt-in, I highly recommend replacing it with something irresistible. And when you do this, you will watch your email list grow.

So, to summarize, you want to create a free gift to go on your website and on social media, and you want it to be irresistible. It should:

1) be something they really want
2) solve a problem for them
3) deliver quick results

Keep it simple; create a PDF document for them to download with Three Tips to... or Five Steps to... and you will be on your way to your 5,000 email addresses.

"Everything we do should come from a
place of service."
#WakeUpCall
@KimberlyMaska

11

You Are Not Serving If You Are Not Selling

"Everything in life is a sale and everything you want is a commission."

~ Grant Cardone

SALES. JUST THE word sales makes us uncomfortable, doesn't it? When we think of a salesman, we envision someone who is pushy, underhanded, and manipulative.

The most popular comment I hear in my Spiritual Biz Bootcamp when we go to talk about sales is, "I don't want to manipulate anyone." I don't want you manipulating anyone either, but I do want you serving.

Have you ever wondered where the judgment about sales people comes from? Why do we connect the word sales with some form of a push person?

To discover the answer, let's first ask the question, *what is sales?* A genuine sale is simply an energy exchange, which is a lovely thing. There should be a balanced energy exchange when you sell something. You provide a service, and you receive compensation in return. So then, we have to ask again, how did an energy exchange ever become negative?

Just how we discussed earlier that money is just energy, it is neither good nor bad, the same holds true with sales. There are good salespeople and bad salespeople. There are positive people and negative people. Your experience around money or sales has to do with the people you engage with. Sales is simply a reflection of the energy of the person doing the selling.

The real problem lies in the fact that most people are not trained to be good at sales. It is bizarre that *anyone* can apply for a sales position. There is no "BA in Sales," no special requirements. That is why you have had negative experiences. The sales people you have encountered haven't a clue what they are doing, so they push and manipulate because it is the only tool they have in their toolbox.

A "bad" salesperson sees a sale as a way to earn a living and cares more about receiving than they do about giving. They do not care if they give less than they receive, and that is why it feels uncomfortable. The energy exchange is out of balance.

As spiritual leaders, you need to make sure that what you are delivering to your clients has a greater value than what you are receiving in the form of energy money. Then the energy exchange is in balance and you know you are serving when you are selling.

We have a course called Spiritual Biz Closer that is taught by my husband, Daniel Pape. But we only allow Bootcamp graduates in the program because it is important for us to know that anyone we teach the techniques of a Spiritual Closer to is giving more than they are receiving.

You see, you have to earn the right to ask for the money. That's very important that you embrace the idea that you have to earn the right to charge. You can be open to receiving what you deserve because you first made sure you're providing a service of value, a quality service, that helps your client achieve their goals.

Serving your clients at the highest level means that they work directly with you so they get access to your energy, and that means enrolling them in one of your programs. To enroll them, you must have an energy exchange, and that means a sale must take place. It's a beautiful thing when you think about it. It's an energy exchange of giving and receiving, and that's really what a business is. The whole point of a business is to give and then receive. We don't have to make it more complicated than it is.

Back to the art of selling, what makes someone a spiritual closer? A spiritual closer F.E.E.L.S. When a spiritual closer is on the phone with a potential client, it isn't about making a sale, it is about serving the client. A spiritual closer has a qualification process in place to make sure they can help the client before they even discuss their program.

I am going to give a tiny crash course on what a spiritual closer would do on a call to a) bring you clarity about how a call should go so it won't feel so uncomfortable and b) give you a few tips you can walk away with so you can begin to serve better. Let's take a closer look at what F.E.E.L.S. stands for.

The F in F.E.E.L.S. stand for "Framing the Call." The goal of this first phase of the call is to establish yourself as the expert who will be guiding them through the call. Framing the call allows the person on the other end of the phone to get a clear picture of how the call will go, which will in turn relax them since there is no confusion on what they should expect. They want someone to guide them, to lead them, to do it kindly and professionally yet with confidence and strength. The benefit is that the client will become comfortable as the process unfolds; gaining trust in you and ultimately enrolling. That's framing the call.

The first E in F.E.E.L.S. stands for "Engage the Client." This is where you take the time to really understand the current situation of the potential client. They have reached out for help, and this is where you have them paint the picture of what is going on in their life. This part of the call is very intimate as they reveal what is keeping them from their joy.

It is very important that they feel comfortable enough to open up and confide in you about what's really going on with them. You can't help them if they're not honest with you or themselves. The benefit of this level of engagement is that they will reveal to you that they can no longer sustain where they are, which will make them the perfect client.

The second E in F.E.E.L.S. stands for "Energize the Client." The goal of energizing them is to show them what life will look like when they find their joy. You do this by visualizing their life after their wound has been healed and their pain has been transcended. The benefit is that they are inspired to wholeheartedly obtain the joyful, meaningful life they deserve. They become inspired and they will see it is not just an option to work with you but a necessity.

The L in F.E.E.L.S. stands for "Level with the Client." Now we switch to being honest with them about where they are in their journey. As an expert, you lay out where they are and the dedication it will take to get to where they want to be. The goal of this process is actually to qualify them.

If you want a high success rate in your business, you need to make sure you are working with the best possible clients. Only after you are sure you can help them and want to work with them will you offer your program. And if you don't think you can help them, tell them. There is nothing shameful about that. It's actually quite refreshing to realize, *look, I just can't help you.*

Here is a key question to qualify a potential client: "How committed are you to solving [THE THING KEEPING THEM FROM THEIR JOY]? Is there anything—money, time, relationships—that would keep you from making this your number one priority?" If they are committed, and nothing will stand in their way, then you can qualify them.

The S in F.E.E.L.S. stands for "Solving the Problem." You only get to this stage if you have qualified them. The goal is to serve them at the highest level and this can only be accomplished by enrolling them into your program. You aren't really serving them if you don't enroll them into a life-changing program. After you qualify them, you present them with the investment opportunity. Notice my phrasing: *Investment Opportunity.* This is an opportunity for them to invest in themselves and heal to change their lives.

Now did any of that feel salesy and uncomfortable? No, of course not. When you become a spiritual closer, you know you are coming from a place of service. And when you are talking to your soul tribe, a discovery call becomes a simple conversation and a decision to work together.

Before we leave this section, I have a funny story to share. Now, when my team is on the phone with someone, and we have qualified them for my Spiritual

Biz Bootcamp, we don't take that lightly. We know Source guided them to us and they have a purpose to fulfill. So we hold them accountable to step up while we are on the call together. Well, a couple of weeks ago, a woman said, "I'm feeling pressured."

And my response was, "Damn straight. You have lives to change, and you aren't serving by staying where you are in your life." It was like a lightbulb went off for her. She paused—I could actually *feel* her energy shift over the phone—and said, "You're right." That shift got her to see the importance of the conversation and the importance of enrolling in Bootcamp so she can share her gifts with the world.

Part of being a spiritual closer is being strong enough to make sure they don't fall into limiting beliefs that will keep them exactly where they are. Letting them sit in a story of, "I don't have any money," or "I don't know if I am ready," isn't serving them at all. The "pressure" is holding them in their highest light, seeing them reaching their full potential. I will apply that kind of pressure any day of the week.

Still feeling a little uncertain about selling? Clear up your resistance around "selling" so you can serve on this planet at the highest level.

Get my Transcending Sales module here:
www.awakeupcallforlightworkers.com

"You aren't serving if you aren't selling."
#WakeUpCall
@KimberlyMaska

12

Your Role In The Paradigm Shift

"The purpose of life is finding the largest burden that can bear and bearing it."

~ Jordan B. Peterson

I HAVE SHARED with you why I believe you are needed to assist the planet in evolving its consciousness during this paradigm shift. For those of you have felt like you don't belong here, on this planet, now you know why you are here.

This is an unprecedented time in history and the planet needs us. We need to hold our vibrations so that we can be living examples for other people. We need to help the people who are sitting in fear—help them raise their vibration and help them reconnect with Source. All of this is happening for a reason, and it's going to be an incredible transformation when it's done.

WHAT YOU NEED IN ORDER TO SERVE NOW

So here's what you need to get out there and serve *now*:

1) You need to check in on your vibration. Are you holding steady? If something is coming up in the form of fear, or a limiting belief, acknowledge it and take some time to heal it.
2) Have a high awareness of the current 3D situation while holding your 5D vibration. You need to remain steady in your vibration during this time of crisis so that you can serve the people who need you the most.
3) Be an alchemist of fear and limiting beliefs. Get your responses ready so that you can maintain your vibration even when those around you are trying to bring yours down.
4) Know that this pandemic is the call to action for Lightworkers. We have been preparing for this for decades with our own awakening process. We are ready.
5) Be 100 percent responsible for you, your vibration, and your income.
6) You must use 3D tools to spread your 5D message. There has to be a full integration of the dimensions.
7) Step out of the 3D by no longer "earning" money but learning to create money through your creative connection with Source.

8) Create a conscious money story that will serve you and your goals. Remove the story that probably didn't even belong to you in the first place, so you can create the abundance you desire.

9) Having a genuine soul connection with your tribe is your key to success. None of the marketing stuff out there will work if you don't have a soul connection with your tribe. If you've been trying a bunch of different programs and can't get them to work, it's because you're missing this piece.

10) Your email list is an asset to your business. Begin to build it now, and you'll see that your greatest level of service comes from your business. Your business is a vehicle to serve.

11) You aren't serving if you aren't selling. Shift your vibration around money so you can serve the souls that are waiting for you.

I have to ask, why did you pick up this book?

- Because you know you have a gift to share, but you need guidance on how to start your spiritual business?
- Because you're tired of your nine to five, and you're ready to be your own boss?
- Because you want to be in charge of your own income?
- Or maybe it's because you want to work from home so you can spend time with your family?
- Maybe it's because Source guided you to step out and you have no other choice?

I actually bet it's all of these, isn't it?

Are you ready to play your role in this paradigm shift? The Coronavirus—this wake-up call for Lightworkers—is happening to force us to step out and serve. That's what happens in a time of crisis.

When a crisis happens, extraordinary people step up and do extraordinary things.

The world needs leaders right now because so many people are in a panic. They are anxious. They are terrified. That is *exactly* why they need us—the Lightworkers of the world who have been preparing emotionally, mentally, spiritually for this moment. They need us STEP OUT NOW to serve and guide them to a place of balance and to reestablish their connection to Source.

If there was ever a time to step out, it is now. There is no time to wait. There's no time to hesitate. There's no time to be in fear of stepping out. There's no more excuses—no more "I don't have time," "I don't have money." The time is now. This Coronavirus has happened as part of our spiritual awakening. It's part of our tests, and it's here to get us to step out and serve. And since many of us are currently quarantined and homebound, it's the perfect time to jumpstart your spiritual business and take control of your own income.

So now I am holding you 100 percent responsible for taking action. Use the "What You Need to Serve NOW" list as a checklist to follow, and let's create miracles together.

Share this message with your fellow Lightworkers so we can assist the planet in evolving its consciousness.

"When a crisis happens, extraordinary people step up and do extraordinary things."
#WakeUpCall
@KimberlyMaska

DON'T WANT TO GO IT ALONE?

You don't have to do this alone. I have built a community of spiritual entrepreneurs working together with the same goal in mind: shifting consciousness on the planet.

In the Resources section of this book, you will find information on the various ways to connect with this community and with me.

Spiritual Biz Bootcamp Success Stories

I AM SO proud of my clients who are out there changing lives every day. Here are just a few beautiful success stories.

> "Bootcamp taught me invaluable, lifelong skills. More importantly, with the support of Kimberly, her team, and my classmates, I had the courage to step out and keep stepping out. I had no idea just how profoundly my life would change.
>
> I am now daily living my dream as a psychic medium and spiritual coach to others. Watching my clients' lives transform forever is an unbelievable blessing. Out of the blue, last fall, Travel Channel reached out to me. I did nothing other than be me, and Hollywood came calling. I'm now a featured expert on an international series.
>
> Two years after graduating Bootcamp, Kimberly is still supportive and my classmates continue to provide a business network like no other. Without a doubt, I would not be where I am without Bootcamp, and I wouldn't be serving clients at this level."
>
> ~ Andres St. Amand

"When I started Spiritual Biz Bootcamp, I had nothing. Now, I have a functioning business, and I am mentoring clients out of difficult times in recovery. Bootcamp gave me the tools and wisdom to create the foundation for my business. In many respects, it gave me a kick up my ass—to make something of my life while helping others.

I feel so blessed to have this opportunity. Addiction makes so many suffer. Many live in a state of fear of their own lives in recovery. Perspective of the mentality is the number one lesson for me. Everything is born to help you; you just have to find that flow.

My life has given me the gift to teach ones who are truly ready to change their lives. I get great pleasure from teaching people in my program 'Recovery to Mastery' as it has changed my life and my clients' lives too."

~ Tommy Legge

"Choosing Kimberly Maska as my mentor has been the absolute greatest blessing I could ever imagine for my spiritually based business. Bootcamp paid for itself two times over within months of graduating because of my clients who signed up to work with me.

Within my first year of business, I gathered over 3,000 people in my tribe who had been asking and praying to receive my specific message to humanity. I am excited to share that I still consistently have about a hundred people joining my group every week!

More than all of the exceptionally successful numbers, I am just the most fulfilled I have ever been.

I am in deep gratitude to have found a spiritual business mentor who is so authentic, so passionate, and who truly cares about me and my success. There are no limits with Kimberly Maska! She sees the big picture of the new consciousness we are creating on the earth. If you feel a resonance with her, I would strongly suggest you consider doing whatever it takes to work with her. Go to Kimberly with confidence."

~ Emily Potter

"My experiences in Spiritual Biz Bootcamp completely transformed my life and business. When I first filled out the application for Bootcamp, I put my income goal as $10k per month—something that I thought was over and beyond what I was capable of achieving at that time. One month into Bootcamp I had my best month yet, and just two months out of Bootcamp, I hit that $10k goal, and the incoming abundance has been a constant for me ever since.

Throughout my time in bootcamp, I learned not only about running a spiritual business but also about what deep inner shifts I needed to master in order to step into my destiny as a spiritual leader on this planet. I couldn't have gotten to where I am today without Kimberly and her team. I am forever grateful that divine destiny brought us together."

~ Ines Heals

Review Request

Welcome to my spiritual family!

The message in this book changes lives.

Share this book with your fellow Lightworkers.

And please, leave an honest review on Amazon.

https://www.kimberlymaska.com/WakeUpCallReview

The more reviews, the more people will hear this message and help accelerate the paradigm shift.

Thank you so much!

RESOURCES

For FREE Tips & Motivation, Follow Kimberly!

Twitter: @kimberlymaska

Facebook: /kimberlymaskaspiritualentrepreneur/

Free Facebook Group: /groups/spiritualbizsuccess/

Instagram: @kimberlymaska

WANT MORE HELP?

Getting started is often the biggest hurdle for spiritual entrepreneurs and authors. You may have read this book only knowing you want to help people but don't know how. I see it every day.

Here are some of the ways I can help you:

A twelve-week transformational program where you experience spiritual expansion and receive all of the tools and coaching you need to create a six-figure spiritual business. This is an intense mentorship where you work directly with me and my team so you can achieve success. www.spiritualbizsuccess.com

A six-week program that we created to prepare you for joining us in Spiritual Biz Bootcamp. You get the first four weeks of Bootcamp content so you can create some momentum in your spiritual biz.

Jump Start

YOUR SPIRITUAL BIZ

A fully automated program containing over thirty training videos that are part of Spiritual Biz Bootcamp. If you are a good self-starter, this could be a good option for you.

www.jumpstartyourspiritualbiz.com

Mastery
SPIRITUAL BIZ

My year-long program for spiritual entrepreneurs dedicated to hitting and crossing the half-million-a-year mark.

Spiritual Biz
C L O S E R

Become a spiritual closer so you can be sure to serve your clients at the highest level by enrolling them into your program.

Spiritual Biz
P U B L I S H I N G

The publisher for authors dedicated to shifting consciousness and who are ready to monetize their books.

Discover us at www.spiritualbizpublishing.com

About the Author

Kimberly Maska is the publisher of Spiritual Biz Magazine, creator of Spiritual Biz Bootcamp, and CEO of Spiritual Biz Publishing.

She uses her business and marketing expertise to show spiritual entrepreneurs how to Make Money While You Meditate™.

She brings twenty years of business development experience to the table, including eight years on Wall Street. Marrying her business expertise with her love for consciously creating life, she shows spiritual coaches how to create financial abundance with their gifts while serving their clients at the highest level.

It is her soul purpose to help 5,000 spiritual entrepreneurs create 5,000 businesses in the next five years.

Kimberly lives in Asheville, NC with her husband, Daniel Pape, and their adorable pug, Bogart.

Made in the USA
Thornton, CO
02/10/23 09:48:42